FOR THE GRANDFATHER WHO HAS EVERYTHING

A Funny Book for Grandfathers

Team Golfwell and Bruce Miller

For the Grandfather Who Has Everything by Bruce Miller and Team Golfwell

FOR THE GRANDFATHER WHO HAS EVERYTHING, A Funny Book for Grandfathers, Copyright © 2022, Pacific Trust Holdings NZ Ltd. All rights reserved for the collective work only. No part of this book may be reproduced or transmitted in any form or by any means, electronic or mechanical, including photocopying, recording, or by any information storage and retrieval system, without written permission from the author, except for brief quotations as would be used in a review.

This is the fifth book in the series, *For Someone Who Has Everything.*

Cover by Queen Graphics. All images are from Creative Commons or Shutterstock

ISBN 9798423279240 (Amazon paperback)

ISBN 9798424827112 (Amazon hardback)

ISBN 9781991161635 (Ingram EPUB)

ISBN 9781991161642 (Ingram paperback)

ISBN 9781991156570 (Ingram hardcover case laminate)

For the Grandfather Who Has Everything by Bruce Miller and Team Golfwell

A Gentleman. "My grandfather was a wonderful role model. Through him I got to know the gentle side of men."

— Sarah Long, English actress, and TV presenter

Age to me means nothing. "I can't get old because I'm working. I felt old when I was twenty-one and out of work.

"As long as you're working, you stay young. When I'm in front of an audience, all that love, and vitality sweeps over me and I forget my age. Grandchildren do the same."

– George Burns

Practical joke reversed. My grandparents married in 1910. They spent their wedding night in my nanna's family home, with her parents and siblings. When they went to bed, my grandpa discovered that someone had attached a cowbell to the underside of the wire sprung bed - presumably to alert all and sundry to any newlywed action.

Grandpa silently removed the bell, so they could enjoy their privacy.

At around 3am, he got out of bed and rang the bell as loud as he could for about 5 minutes.

-- Anon.

Baby wonderment. "Having a baby changes the way you view your in-laws. I love it when they come to visit now. They can hold the baby and I can go out."

-- Matthew Broderick, Actor, Golden Globe nominee.

If I'd known I was going to live this long, I'd have taken better care of myself. Those who love deeply never grow old; they may die of old age, but they die young. And the idea is to die young as late as possible.

-- Anon.

Awesome grandchild: "Grandpa, what does it feel like to have an awesome grandchild?"

For the Grandfather Who Has Everything by Bruce Miller and Team Golfwell

Grandpa: "I don't know. I should have asked your great-great grandfather."

You just know. "You know you're a grandparent when you laugh when your grandkids do the same things that made you so angry when your kids did them."

-- Unknown

Boo! "To a small child, the perfect granddad is unafraid of big dogs and fierce storms but acts absolutely terrified when the child says the word 'boo!'"

— Robert Breault

Patience. "One thing you always taught me grandfather is that patience is better than anything, there is no reason to rush in life, better things come with patience."

-- Nicole Gopher Mampuya, "The Appreciation"

Memories. "My Grandpa died when I was very young. He was from Romania, and I didn't understand a lot of his jokes and he like many others used to laugh before he got to the end of them.

He appreciated poop jokes and could recite major portions of Macbeth from memory. He adored my grandma who was younger than him.

His bad back was cured forever when my dad and his siblings put some eels in a bucket that he stepped in one morning on vacation upstate and he flipped out. He stretched in all the right ways while swearing at and chasing his kids.

As his grandson, I have lost count of all the inappropriate things I've done and said -- and I'm not that old. I wonder who will keep track of me one day?"

-- Anon.

Hands. "One of the most powerful handclasps is that of a new grandbaby around the finger of a grandfather."

For the Grandfather Who Has Everything by Bruce Miller and Team Golfwell

— Joy Hargrove

House rules. Grandson: "Grandpa, can I have a piece of candy?"

Grandpa: "What's the rule in this house?"

Grandson: "No candy until after dinner."

Grandpa: "No, that's grandma's rule. Grandpa's rule is, bring me one too."

"I love this child... Red-haired — patient and gentle like her mother — fey and funny like her father. When she giggles, I can hear her father when he and I were young. I am part of this child. It may be only because we share genes and that therefore smell familiar to each other.... It may be that a part of me lives in her in some important way.... But for now, it's jellybeans and 'Old MacDonald' that unite us."

-- Robert Fulghum, Author

Kicked it. "My grandfather left to go Christmas shopping while my wife decorated the house, and he came back empty-handed 45 minutes later. I asked what happened, and he told me he pooped his pants at the mall and the turd fell out of his pants leg!

I asked him what he did about it, and he said, 'I kicked it and kept walking.'"

    -- Anon.

Grandpa's ears. "Grandpa has ears that truly listen, arms that always hold, love that's never-ending, and a heart that's made of gold."

    -- Unknown

Lots of fun. "The simplest toy, one which even the youngest child can operate, is called a grandparent."

    — Sam Levenson

No control. My granddad asked me how to print on his computer. I told him it's Ctrl-P. He said he hasn't been able to do that for ages.

-- Unknown

A brief and interesting history of grandfather. "My grandfather ran away from home when he was 16. Worked in a factory for about a year, bought a car, drove most of the way to Miami, ditched the car when it broke down, and took the bus the rest of the way there.

Once in Miami, he started working as a pool boy at one of the hotels on the beach. One day his friend showed up on a motorbike/scooter. The lifeguard supervisor asked my grandpa why he didn't have his own scooter and he said it was because he didn't have $220. So, his boss pulled out a wad of cash, handed him $220, and told him to get a scooter.

"But I can't pay you back"

"Oh, you'll pay me back"

And that's the story of how my grandfather became a runner for the mob in Miami Beach in the 50s

His supervisor at the hotel was a bookie and had my grandfather buy the scooter so he could run around collecting money for him. I guess all the older lifeguards and managers (and probably up to the owners) at the hotels in Miami Beach at the time had ties to the mob. He said he was able to pay off the scooter loan within a few weeks so that gives you an idea of the kind of money that was going through there.

My grandfather quit at the end of the summer and went to join the navy, where he eventually became one of the first underwater demo team members in the SEALS and was part of the rescue team who intercepted Apollo 11 when it landed in the Pacific. He donated a lot of his memorabilia to the Navy SEAL Museum in Ft Pierce, Fl."

-- Anon.

Strong will. "Don't ever, ever underestimate the will of a grandfather... we got here before you and we will be here after you."

-- Martin Sheen

Lots of energy. "Do you know why grandchildren are always so full of energy? They suck it out of their grandparents. You might have read, 'and on the seventh day God rested.' His grandchildren must have been out of town."

-- Gene Perret

Magician. "Grandfathers are like magicians. They can create wonderful memories for their grandchildren out of thin air."

-- Anon.

Grandpa is texting his son.

Grandpa: Ok to visit tonight? Have some things I want to drop off you and the girls.

Son: Sure thing. You gonna bang gram?

Grandpa: Would like to but she closed up shop years ago.

Son: OMG, I meant Are you going to bring gram.

Grandpa: Figured that. Don't give yourself a heart attack. Gran is coming if she can stop laughing by then.

For the Grandfather Who Has Everything by Bruce Miller and Team Golfwell

-- Anon

Always have time. "Grandpas always have time for you when everyone else is too busy."

-- Anon.

A grandpa wedding story. Sometimes you must make the best out of a bad situation. At a relatives wedding, my grandpa's suspenders snapped, and his pants fell down around his ankles. But instead of immediately pulling them back up, he asked very loudly if anyone wanted to take a picture first."

-- Anon.

Grandpa and Teen texting.

Teen: GRANDPAAA! I'm pregnant!!!

Grandpa: Are you drunk?

Teen: Yeah. why?

Grandpa: You're a boy.

For the Grandfather Who Has Everything by Bruce Miller and Team Golfwell

Blend. A lovely blend. "Grandfathers are a delightful blend of laughter, caring deeds, wonderful stories and love."

-- Anon.

Frugal. "My grandpa's so cheap, when he dies, he'll probably walk towards the light – to turn it off."

--Anon.

Happy Anniversary! I sent an anniversary card to my grandparents on their 54th anniversary and wrote, "Happy Anniversary you lovebirds!" and my grandpa later sent me this text message,

"Thanks, Tony, for the card. Yes, I love birds. I feed them in the winter and put out a birdbath in the summer. Grandpa"

A perfect blend. "The very old and the very young have something in common that makes it right that they should be left alone together. Dawn and sunset see stars shining in a blue sky; but morning and midday and afternoon do not, poor things."

— Elizabeth Goudge

Ripping advice. "Make up your mind to this. If you are different, you are isolated, not only from people of your own age but from those of your parents' generation and from your children's generation too. They'll never understand you and they'll be shocked no matter what you do. But only your grandfather would be proud of you and say, 'There's a chip off the old block,' and your grandchildren will sigh enviously and say, 'What an old rip Grandpa must have been!' and they'll try to be like you."

— Margaret Mitchell

Grandpa Poem. As a little girl, I followed your steps,

We ate butter and crackers by the fire

At night.

You loved to make me smile, you said I was your guiding light.

For the Grandfather Who Has Everything by Bruce Miller and Team Golfwell

We went fishing, and filled up the pail,

As soon as we arrived home,

You bragged, "Look at all the fish she caught."

You made me feel so proud.

You said I was smart, pretty, and so kind,

So, I grew up that way,

Thanks to you, Grandpa,

A quiet fiercely loving man so kind.

As I grew older, and we had coffee

At the kitchen table, and troubles were on my mind,

You would grin and say, "You don't have to

Carry the world upon your shoulders, babe,

Now tell me what's wrong, and part of that world is mine."

-- Unknown

Am I a bad grandpa? Really? Am I bad just because I gave the kids chocolate-covered coffee beans before sending them home?

-- Anon.

Miss him. "I miss him still today. My grandfather. His long, whiskery eyebrows, his huge hands and hugs, his warmth, his prayers, his stories, but above all his shining example of how to live and how to die."

— Bear Grylls, excerpt from "Mud, Sweat and Tears"

Rolex. An old Italian man is dying. He calls his grandson to his bedside and says, "Guido, I wanna you lissina me. I wanna you to take-a-my chrome plated .38 revolver so you will always remember me."

"But grandpa, I really don't like guns. How about you leave me your Rolex watch instead?"

"You lissina me, boy. Somma day you gonna be runna da business, you gonna have a beautiful wife, lotsa money, a big-a home and maybe a couple of bambinos. Somma day you gonna come-a home and maybe finda you wife inna bed with another man. Whatta you gonna do then? Pointa to you watch and say, 'times up'?"

No regrets. "You will never look back on life and think, 'I've spent too much time with my grandchildren.'"

    -- Anon.

If it's breaks – get grandpa. "Grandfathers are for loving and fixing things."

    -- Anon.

10 again. "Grandparents enjoy most the company of their grandchildren. For with them, they experience the miracle of being 10 again."

    — Meeta Ahluwalia, Author

For the Grandfather Who Has Everything by Bruce Miller and Team Golfwell

It was grandpa's 100th birthday and he was 100% fit and in perfect health. He was asked how he lived so long?

He said, "I have a long life because I spend so much time outdoors. I've been in the open-air taking walks rain or shine every day for the last 75 years."

"Grandpa, how did you manage to maintain such a rigorous fitness routine?

"Very simple. When grandma and I got married 75 years ago we made solemn pledge that whenever we had a disagreement, whoever was proved to be wrong would go outside and take a long walk."

-- Anon.

Revolt. "Every generation revolt against its fathers and makes friends with its grandfathers."

– Lewis Mumford

Ask Grandma. "My grandson is sharp. He knows if Mom says no, he asks Grandma. If Grandma says no…, Wait, who am I kidding? Grandma never says no."

For the Grandfather Who Has Everything by Bruce Miller and Team Golfwell

-- Unknown

Wrong one! "My mom had to work late one day, so she asked grandpa to pick up my infant brother from daycare. Well, when my grandpa returned home and put the infant carrier down, and we all gasped at the same time. He had brought the WRONG KID home from daycare!"

The worst part was the baby he brought home was tan with black hair, while my infant brother was blonde!

-- Anon.

Rodney Dangerfield. "At Christmas time we couldn't afford tinsel, so we'd wait till grandpa sneezed."

—Rodney Dangerfield

What did you do in the old days? A grandson asked his grandfather what his great-grandfather did in the old days before TV.

Grandad replied, "Oh they had radio and did other things."

"But just listening to the radio is boring," the grandson said. "What else did they do?"

"I'm not exactly sure. You should ask your 16 aunts and uncles if they know."

No glasses. My grandpa is 95 years old and doesn't use glasses. He drinks straight from the bottle.

-- Henny Youngman

Made by God. A little girl was sitting on her granddad's lap while he read her a story. She kept taking her eyes off the book and reaching up and touching his old, wrinkled face. After a few times doing this, she finally asked, "Grandpa, were you made by God?"

"Yes, dear," he replied. "I was made by God a long time ago."

The little girl paused for a moment and then asked, "And did God make me?"

"Of course, dear." replied her grandfather. "God made you not long ago."

The girl felt her own face and then her granddad's again, thought for a moment, and then said, "God's getting better at it, isn't he?"

    -- Unknown

The wait is over. "I'm going to be your grandpa! I have the biggest smile. I've been waiting to meet you for such a long, long while."

    -- Billy Crystal

Walk the walk. "You never know the love of a grandparent until you become one."

    -- Anon.

Dentist office. I took my grandpa to the dentist near our new house and had a severe toothache. He filled out the paperwork fast so the dentist could look at him as quickly as possible and checked "None" in each health section. There was also a section that says you can write any other medical or health issues you may have, and he left that completely blank.

The dentist had my grandpa quickly seated in the dental chair and rapidly reviewed the paperwork. Then he stepped on the floor button to begin tilting the dental chair backward. My grandpa jumped up right out of the chair howling. The dentist said, "What, what's wrong?"

Grandpa says, "I think my colostomy bag just emptied out."

The dentist says, "Why didn't you put that on your health form?"

Grandpa says, "Oh, because I don't really need it anymore, I just like having one."

Stories. "All grandfathers possess a limitless number of interesting stories gathered from the past."

-- Unknown

Horses. "To be content, horse people need only a horse, or, lacking that, someone else who loves horses with whom they can talk. It was always that way with my grandfather.

He took me places just so we could see horses, be near them. We went to the circus and the rodeo at Madison Square Garden. We watched parades down Fifth Avenue. Finding a horse, real or imagined, was like finding a dab of magic potion that enlivened us both.

Sometimes I'd tell my grandfather about all the horses in my elaborate dreams. He'd lean over, smile, and assure me that, one day, I'd have one for real. And if my grandfather, my Opa, told me something was going to come true, it always did."

— Allan J. Hamilton, Zen Mind, Zen Horse: The Science and Spirituality of Working with Horses

What grandfathers do. Grandpa teaches you what Sundays are about - football and yelling at the TV. He always gives you an extra scoop of ice cream. They are just like dads, only they have no rules, and they always give you the best bedtime snacks.

-- Unknown

Paying attention. "My grandfather taught me how important it is to have your eyes open, because you never know what's going to come your way."

– Bobbi Brown, Founder Bobbi Brown Cosmetics

How old are you? When my grandson asked me how old I was, I teasingly replied, "I'm not sure."

"Look in your underwear, Grandpa," he advised "Mine says I'm 4 to 6."

-- Anon.

How the heck did I get this old! "It's weird being the same age as old people. My mind thinks it is the same as it was when I was young."

-- Anon.

A joke. Two grandmothers, very loving and faithful wives, went out for a girls' night and got a little overzealous with the margaritas. They stayed out late, and on their walk home realized they both needed to pee. By that time, everything was closed, but they were walking past a graveyard and figured it was secluded enough. They each picked a shadowy grave and popped a squat.

One of the ladies, upon realizing she had nothing to wipe with, pulled off her panties and used those. The other was next to a grave with a wreath on it, so she pulled off the ribbon and wiped herself with that.

The next day, one grandpa called the other. It was well past noon, and both women were still in bed, hungover. "These girls' nights have to stop," he said, "My wife came home with no panties last night."

"You think that's bad?" the other replied, "My wife came home with a card stuck to her ass that said, 'From all of us at the fire department: Thanks for everything! We'll never forget you!'"

Story keepers. "Grandfathers are the keepers of the story, and they help reinforce lessons of the parents while providing yet a different perspective."

    -- Bill High

Transition. "A baby has a way of making a man out of his father and a boy out of his grandfather."

    -- Angie Papadakis

Distance? "There is no distance that can lessen a grandparent's love."

-- Anon.

Grandchildren survey. A group of 7-year-old grandchildren was asked to say what grandparents are. Here are a few of their answers.

- Grandparents don't have to do anything except be there when we come to see them. They are so old they shouldn't play hard or run. It is good if they drive us to the shops and give us money.

- When they take us for walks, they slow down past things like pretty leaves and caterpillars.

- They show us and talk to us about the color of the flowers and also why we shouldn't step on "cracks."

- They don't say, "Hurry up."

- Usually, grandmothers are fat but not too fat to tie your shoes.

- They wear glasses and funny underwear.

- They can take their teeth and gums out.

- Grandparents don't have to be smart.

- They can answer questions like, "Why isn't God married?" and "How come dogs chase cats?"

- When they read to us, they don't skip. They don't mind if we ask for the same story over again.

- Everybody should try to have a grandmother, especially if you don't have a television, because they are the only grown-ups who like to spend time with us.

- They know we should have snack-time before bedtime, and they say prayers with us every time and kiss us even when we've acted badly.

- One was asked where his grandma lived. "Oh," he said, "She lives at the airport and when we want her, we just go get her. Then when we're done having her visit, we take her back to the airport."
- Grandpa is the smartest man on earth! He teaches me good things, but I don't get to see him enough to get as smart as him! [1]

Experience. "A grandfather has the wisdom of long experience and the love of an understanding heart."

    -- Unknown

Influence. "My grandfather has a big influence on me; without him, I wouldn't be where I am now."

– Angelique Kerber, Former World No. 1 Tennis

No thank you. True story. "My grandfather would buy a bottle of cough medicine and empty it. Then without rinsing the bottle, he would fill it with brandy. He gave me a sip when I was a teen. To this day, I still can't drink brandy."

-- Anon.

Close friends. "The closest friends I made all through life have been people who also grew up close to a loved and loving grandmother or grandfather."

– Margaret Mead

True story. "My grandfather was a Reverend of the Presbyterian Church until he retired. When I was small my mother and I lived with him and my grandmother. So, although my mother wasn't religious and I really wasn't at a young age, we attended church to see him.

Basically, it was always hilarious because my grandfather would be up there, yelling about the evils of the Devil. Then,

I'd frantically wave at him from the back, and his face would change to a smile, and he'd wave back before immediately switching back to Reverend mode.

All this led to some funny moments and the churchgoers having a good laugh when I'd insist on going up to see him and he'd have to stand and do his church speech while holding me."

    -- Anon.

Seriously, "Grandparents should play the same role in the family as an elder statesman can in the government of a country. They have the experience and knowledge that comes from surviving a great many years of life's battles and the wisdom, hopefully, to recognize how their grandchildren can benefit from this."

    — Geoff Dench

Antiques. "Grandpas are just little antique boys."

    -- Unknown

Self-respect. "Self-respect is something that our grandparents, whether or not they had it, knew all about.

They had instilled in them when they were young a certain discipline -- the sense that one lives by doing things one does not particularly want to do, by putting fears and doubts to one side, by weighing immediate comforts against the possibility of larger, even intangible, comforts."

— Joan Didion

Grandfathers just know. "Grandfathers are better than CSI. He knows you did it, he knows how you did it, and he can hear you trying to hide the evidence."

-- Unknown

Got to go. True story by a grandson.

"My grandparents lived in on a farm in an old house with one bedroom on the first floor and the bathroom on the second floor and in the basement.

I had to sleep on the couch when I visited.

Grandpa always got up at night to take a pee off the back porch – and he'd be buck naked – even if it was 10 below outside.

-- Anon.

God does have a sense of humor. "We grow up opposing our parents only to become like them enough to oppose our children who behave as we once did — a reminder of how dreadful we were toward those now-vindicated grandparents. And you thought God had no sense of humor."

— Richelle E. Goodrich

Sounds. "The sound of my grandkids laughing is my favorite sound in the world. The sound of them sleeping is a close second!"

-- Anon.

Granddad joke. My grandfather's last wish was to have his remains cremated and convert his ashes into a diamond.

That's a lot of pressure!

Giving them a sense of identity. Here is a list of things you may want to talk to your grandkids about.

For the Grandfather Who Has Everything by Bruce Miller and Team Golfwell

Who in the family were named after other relatives and why?

Tell them where you were born and what it was like then. What was your parents' home like and where in the house or yard did you play?

Tell them about your favorite teachers in school.

What did you do for fun when you were small?

Did you have a best friend? What was he like?

Did your parents give you a weekly allowance? What did you spend your money on?

How did you meet grandma?

How did you propose to her? Talk about your wedding.

You can also tell them about what you wanted to be when you grew up and why.

When did you get your first car?

Tell them about your grandparents.

Tell them about the day their mom or dad was born.

Did you have a pet? A favorite toy?

What are you thankful for?

For the Grandfather Who Has Everything by Bruce Miller and Team Golfwell

Meaning. "Grandparents are a delightful blend of laughter, caring deeds, wonderful stories, and love. Grandfather means a best, crazy, and an old friend forever who will never cheat or leave you. He's a guy who finds both joy and peace in his heart each time a new grandchild is born."

—Unknown

Riddles for smart grandkids. Something to share with grandchildren and get them thinking...

A man walks into an art museum and stares at a painting. A guard walks up and asks him why he is so interested in the painting he responds with, "Brothers and sisters I have none, but that man's father is my father's son."

Who is the man in the painting?

A. The man in the painting is his son.

Which one of your grandpa's boys is not your uncle?

A. Your Dad

Two fathers and two sons go fishing together in the same boat. They all catch a fish but the total catch for the day is three fish. How is this possible?

A. There are three men, 1) a grandfather, 2) a father (the grandfather's son) and 3) the father's son. That is, one of the 'fathers' is also a grandfather. Therefore, the other father is both a son and a father to the grandson. In other words, the one father is both a son and a father.

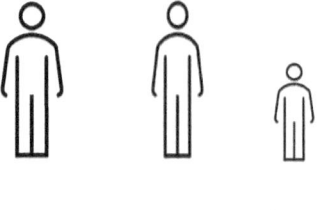

This might be a tough one. How old is Johnny? Johnny is the same age as the number of weeks of his father's age treated as days. And he is the same age as his grandfather's age in months. All three of their ages add up to 120 years.

How old are Johnny, his father, and his grandfather?

A. Johnny is 6. His father is 42 years old since 42 days = 6 weeks. The grandfather is 72 years old since 72 months = 6 years.

Johnny's age is the number of weeks of his father's age treated as days and his grandfather's age in months. All three of their ages add up to 120 years.

For the Grandfather Who Has Everything by Bruce Miller and Team Golfwell

Which month has 28 days?

A. All of them.

Grandfather goes out for an afternoon bicycle ride. He rides for one hour at five miles an hour, then three hours at four miles an hour, and finally two hours at seven miles an hour. How many miles did he ride in total?

A. 31 miles.

1 hour at 5 mph = 5 miles

3 hours at 4 mph = 12 miles

2 hours at 7 mph = 14 miles

5 + 12 + 14 = 31 miles

Definition of FUNPA. Like grandpa only cooler. Smarter than dad and surprisingly good-looking. Professional advice giver, family historian, expert storyteller, and spoiler of grandchildren. Helps grandchildren get into mischief they haven't thought of yet. He knows everything and if he doesn't know, he'll make stuff up. He's the World's greatest grand farter – eh, I mean grandfather.

-- Anon.

Experience. "Parents know a lot, but grandparents know everything."

– Unknown

How many grandparents are in the US? There are 70 million grandparents in the US. There are also 2.6 million grandparents who are the primary caregivers of their grandchildren.

President Jimmy Carter signed into law "Grandparents Day" which is legally the first Sunday after Labor Day and heavily promoted online.

Grandparents spend an average of about $2,400 per year mainly for toys for grandchildren. Of all age groups, grandparents are the best off financially than other age groups. [2]

What children need most. "What children need most are the essentials that grandparents provide in abundance. They give unconditional love, kindness, patience, humor, comfort, lessons in life. And, most importantly, cookies."

-- Rudolph Giuliani

Nature's way. "It is one of nature's ways that we often feel closer to distant generations than to the generation immediately preceding us."

– Igor Stravinsky

Some warm thoughts. "Grandfathers have a really tough time saying no to their granddaughters." -- Anon

"Grandpa, you made my childhood unforgettable. I love you." – Anon

"Perfect love sometimes does not come until the first grandchild." -- Welsh proverb

Grandkids remember grandpa's diet.

- "We'd be at the breakfast table and my papa would sit down and eat spoonful's of butter dipped in sugar."

- "Mine would take an old pickle jar and fill it with mashed potatoes and take it for lunch when he went to his factory job every day."

- "My grandpa would be chewing Copenhagen while eating spoonful's of homemade horseradish."

- "Grandfather would drive miles out of town to buy butter sold in 3-pound tubs. He'd put so much butter on his bread you could see his teeth marks after he took a bite."

- "My grandma would make a large family salad bowl and at the end of dinner, gramps would lift the bowl and chug the leftover dressing full of onions, tomato seeds and other stuff. He let out a big belch and slap his belly before wiping his mouth on his sleeve (and fart the rest of the night)."

- "Grandfather hardly ever came in the kitchen. One day he came home early from golf and found a can of beef stew in the refrigerator. He heated it up and ate it. When my grandmother came home, she told him he'd just eaten the dog food."

- "My grandpa would mix all his favorite cereals together in one big jug. Then he'd put rolls of cash in an empty muesli box because in his opinion, 'Muesli is trash, and no one would look there.'"

- "Grandfather was a cattle rancher. He would buy ground beef in the store and open the package in the car on the way home and eat it and claim it was crap compared to the beef cattle he raised on his ranch."

- "We were cleaning out his fridge and he found a jar of tartar sauce with an expiration date of 1974 (this was in the 90s). He scraped off the mold and other stuff and announce, 'Still good!' It is still in his fridge."

- "My grandpa ate onions like apples and fried chicken TV dinners every Friday night. If we went out to a restaurant on a Friday, he would bring along a fried chicken TV dinner and ask the restaurant to heat it up."

- "Grandad would always eat a slice of bologna after eating cake or pie -- "Didn't want the sweet taste in his mouth!"

- "My grandfather would eat heads of garlic like they were apples. One time grandma asked him, 'Did you eat the whole head of garlic?' He answered, 'Well, yeah. But I had a piece of gum afterward. Can you still tell?'"

On the other side of the coin. How I plan not to become a grandparent. I'm going to name my only daughter, "Pregnant." So, when a boy asks her name, he's on his way after he hears, "I'm…" (I'm not sure if that will work?)

    -- Anon.

Identity. "Grandkids love stories and family stories. They may want to learn about how their parents grew up, where their relatives came from, tough times gone through, and relatives they may never have met.

Grandparents often are the source of treasured stories and photos of family. Your stories give them a sense of belonging and can help them appreciate where they fit into your family's history. It becomes a part of their identity formation." [3]

Friend. "A grandpa is a little bit parent, a little bit teacher, and a little bit best friend."

    – Unknown

For the Grandfather Who Has Everything by Bruce Miller and Team Golfwell

Choosing grandpa names.

- G-Dog. For the super-cool grandpas out there to bring out the smiles.

- Grand dude. Talk about another very non-traditional, fun choice—this name can remind any grandpa that age is just a number!

- G-Pa. Some grandparents, like Lionel Richie, go by this shortened version of "grandpa," pronounced "gee-pa."

- Abuelo. This is the Spanish word for "grandpa."

- Gramps. Ideal for laid-back grandpas.

- Gumpa. For the little ones who can't yet say their Rs.

- Ace

- Boss

- Captain

- Champ

- Chief

- Nonno. Italian word for "grandpa.

- Opa. German for grandpa.

- Chief. Great name for the patriarch.

- Pépé. French nickname for grandpa.

- Grandpère. The formal French name for grandpa.

- Coach

- Duke

- Granite

- King

- Saba. Hebrew for grandpa.

- Tutu. Hawaiian. Used for both genders.

- Avo. Portuguese. Used for both genders.

- Skipper

- Babu. Grandpa in Swahili.

- Farfar. Swedish grandpa. Morfar is the Swedish maternal grandfather.

- Papi. Spanish and used for dads and grandads. Popular for a grandad who is more of a father figure.

- Yéye. Mandarin for paternal grandfather.

- Zaida/Zayda. Yiddish for grandfather.

A philosophical view of maturity. "A man's maturity consists in having found again the seriousness one had as a child, at play."

— Friedrich Nietzsche

Outrageous stuff. Did you ever say outrageous things to your grandkids? Here are just a few we've come across. Even though most everyone may say these, we aren't sure why any grandchild would attribute these to granddads. Anyway, we'll let you decide if you've ever said these,

"It's not a salad without bacon."

"You can pick your friends, and you can pick your nose, but you can't pick your friend's nose."

"It's not a party until someone sh#ts their pants."

"You betcha!"

"It's hotter than two possums f@#kin' in a wool sock out here."

"That's slicker than 2 turds in a colostomy bag."

"I'm as tired as a one-legged man in an ass kicking competition."

"I'm going upstairs to give it to your grandma."

"I see, I see, said the blind man to the deaf guy." (Grandson says he's now started saying it himself).

"I was the smartest kid in class. Want to know how? I was the only kid in class."

For anything that takes longer than normal, my granddad would say, "It's like wipin' your butt with a wagon wheel. There ain't no end to it."

When grandpa was asked if he wanted to be buried or cremated, he would always say, "Surprise me!"

Beaten to death. My grandpa was recently beaten to death by my grandma. No not with a rolling pin, she just passed away first.

For the Grandfather Who Has Everything by Bruce Miller and Team Golfwell

-- Anon

Forever young. "To keep the heart unwrinkled, to be hopeful, kindly, cheerful, reverent that is to triumph over old age."

— Thomas Bailey Aldrich

Magic happens. Something magical happens when parents turn into grandparents. Their attitude changes from "money doesn't grow on trees" to spending it like it does.

-- Paul Linden

Teen is amazed. "Today I argued with my grandpa over how old I was for over 15 minutes!"

…"I lost."

-- Unknown

Love grows with age. Just as wisdom grows with age, so does a grandparent's love, and although they may not be there every day, their love and influence are.

Grandchildren should know they were dreamt of lovingly before ever being born, and no one will ever love you like your grandparent.

-- Unknown

The average age of grandparents is on the rise. Children seem to be waiting longer before they decide to begin a family. Years ago, the average age was in the high 40s and now the average age is 50. By the age of 65, almost 96% are grandparents. The average number of grandchildren is 4 to 5. [4]

The good news is since we are living longer now, 70 % of 8-year- old children will have a living great-grandparent! [5]

Getting older. "You know you're getting old when the candles cost more than the cake."

— *Bob Hope*

"I'm at an age when my back goes out more than I do."

— *Phyllis Diller*

"You know you're getting old when you get that one candle on the cake. It's like, 'See if you can blow this out."

— *Jerry Seinfeld*

"I've learned that life is like a roll of toilet paper. The closer it gets to the end, the faster it goes."

— *Andy Rooney*

For the Grandfather Who Has Everything by Bruce Miller and Team Golfwell

"So far, this is the oldest I've been."

— **George Carlin**

"By the time a man is wise enough to watch his step, he's too old to go anywhere."

— **Billy Crystal**

"As you get older, the pickings get slimmer, but the people sure don't."

— **Carrie Fisher**

"You know you're getting older when you're told to slow down by your doctor, instead of by the police."

— **Joan Rivers**

Special place. "Grandfathers do have a special place in the lives of their children's children. They can delight and play with them and even indulge them in ways that they did not indulge their own children.

Grandfather knows that after the fun and games are over with his adorable grandchildren he can return to the quiet of his own home and peacefully reflect on this phenomenon of fatherhood."

-- Alvin F. Poussaint

Well, now that I think about it. "I was around nineteen or so, bragging to my grandpa about going to parties and drinking. He'd been a navigator in WWII, stationed in Italy for much of it.

'I never had any vices,' he told me. 'The other guys would drink, smoke, gamble, but I kept clean. Never had any part of it.'

And then, after a moment's consideration he said, 'Well, actually, I did have one vice...I used to pimp women.'"

-- Anon.

Perfect, of course! "If your baby is 'beautiful and perfect, never cries or fusses, sleeps on schedule and burps on demand, an angel all the time,' you're the grandpa."

— Teresa Bloomingdale

You know you're a grandpa when... You used to get angry at your kids and now you laugh when your grandkids do the same thing. Or,

- You thought you were too old to fall in love again, then your grandchild was born.

- When you hold a baby in your arms and realize the miracle started with you and grandma.

- When you feel the most powerful hand clasp of the first grandbaby around your finger.

- When no one else can tell you what to do except your granddaughter.

- When your grandchildren look up to you no matter how tall they are.

- When joy happens when you enter their room.

Grandma's game. "I remembered how I used to ask my grandma to play a game and she said, 'Let's play who falls asleep first,' and turned away."

-- Anon

It's in the genes. "They say genes skip generations. Maybe that's why grandparents find their grandchildren so likeable."

— Joan McIntosh

A granddaughter's story. "Two nights before our wedding, my then fiancée took me to my grandparents' home, to pick up a beautiful negligee my grandmother had made me for our wedding night. It was truly stunning, and I was so excited.

We both came from devout Catholic families, back then that MEANT abstaining until marriage. So, as you can imagine, at almost 22 and 23 years of age, with our wedding night 2 sleeps away, we were pretty much counting the seconds!

My grandparents then said they had wonderful news! Immediately after the wedding, Papa is going fishing/camping for a week and wants my fiancée to go with him.

My grandmother added, "That leaves you free darling to come to the two operas and the ballet we discussed, with me! Isn't that wonderful!!"

I nearly swallowed my tongue. We both froze like deer in headlights and just looked at each other. I swear my fiancée's eyes were screaming, "Tell me they're joking?"

Then I realized they weren't joking! How on God's green earth is a good Catholic granddaughter, supposed to explain to her totally naive, grandparents that she wants to stay home and have sex with her new husband, not go to the ballet. Or that my new husband may well divorce this good Catholic girl on our wedding night if I suggest he go fishing!?

I had to respond, so I simply said, "that is such a lovely thought, but honestly after all the build up to the wedding etc. we are truly exhausted. By the time our wedding day is done, we really just need to just go to our new home and go to bed."

Yeah, a little deceptive, but not a lie. My fiancée kept shaking his head, asking, "Really, they really were serious? Really?"

This story has brought up some wonderful memories of two people I love and miss very much."

-- LW

Advise. Grandfather's advice to his children. "Wait a few years before you have children so you can just focus on each other, and you don't have anything else to worry about. If you want to go on a vacation, you go. If you want to have sex in the afternoon, you do!"

    -- Unknown

Consolation from the strong. "The best place to be when you're sad is Grandpa's lap."

    -- Unknown

Having a grandpa is the Lord's way of making sure a grandson always has a best friend.

    -- Unknown

Tell me a story. "Grandma and Grandpa, tell me a story and snuggle me with your love. When I'm in your arms, the world seems small, and we're blessed by the heavens above."

    — Laura Spiess

Smoking. My grandad would always say this about smoking, "I knew a lad who smoked 40 a day, and he was never ill a day in his life!

"But he died when he was 21."

-- Anon

Hindsight. "Not a tenth of us who are in business are doing as well as we could if we merely followed the principles that were known to our grandfathers."

– William Feather

Exceptional. "Being an exceptional grandfather is not about changing your grandkids. It is about changing yourself."

– Richard Eyre, Film director

Reaching out. "Because grandparents are usually free to love and guide and befriend the young without having to take daily responsibility for them, they can often reach out past pride and fear of failure and close the space between generations."

– Jimmy Carter, Former US President

Youthful inside. "A grandparent is old on the outside, but young on the inside."

-- Unknown

Pouring whiskey. "Grandma and Grandad also used to ask me to pour their whisky for them, when they babysat for me. I can't have been more than 6 or 7 when I started pouring their whisky, sneaking up the amount because it made them exclaim that No! They shouldn't! And then they would have a massive grin on their faces when I handed it to them.

My Grandma and Grandad were brilliant people, salt of the Earth. They fought in the war, they were poor and had a tough life. I saw them a lot, every week while I was growing up. I loved them both very much, they've been gone 20 years and I still miss them."

-- Unknown

Grandma's confession. "My grandson just asked me if I'm pregnant so I'm starting my diet tomorrow.

-- Anon.

Feel loved. "A grandfather makes us laugh, makes us feel safe, and always makes us feel loved."

– Kate Summers

Grandparents' kissing and hugging. "Every summer we would spend two weeks at my grandparent's home by the beach and a large park. Each evening we'd all get together for something to eat and then go to the park where a lot of retirees would gather for the evening.

Once the drinks were flowing my gran would go into the bedroom and put one of her bikinis on, she'd start this big song and dance about going out to meet one of her boyfriends at the park.

She was the right picture! Lips covered in bright red lipstick, bright white and black polka dot bikini, six-inch heels, big Hollywoodize sunglasses, and sun hat to top it all off.

In this quite lovely but (as I thought back then) not age-appropriate get-up, gran would march up and down and ready to go to the park as if it was some sort of catwalk announcing, "Right kids, I'm off to see one of my many boyfriends; don't wait up!"

My sisters and I would be upset that she would do this to our grandad, we'd be shouting and balling. "Don't go gran! Please don't go, what about grandad?"

My grandad would chirp in as she started to go to the park. "Aye, Peggeeee, don't you want another drink before you go?"

Of course, she'd always stop and have a drink and not end up going. It turns out, it was all just a little act they liked to play out in front of us. My parents would play along with it too…

The outfit gran would be wearing was highly embarrassing. But the most embarrassing part would be when my grandparents would share an old persons' kissing and hugging pretending, they had made up and again it was all done in good fun.

I can't believe how many times we all fell for it. I love them both very much but after they had a few drinks, I wouldn't wish that sight on anyone. ☺

I love them and miss them both very much. RIP."

  -- Fred

Reflections. "Grandpa got us up early, otherwise we might miss something. Sunsets, he loved 'em. Made us love 'em."

  – Lucille Ball

Let me tell you about my grandchildren! "No cowboy was ever faster on the draw than a grandparent pulling a baby picture out of a wallet."

  -- Unknown

My dad told me this story about my grandfather. Back in the '50s the roads were not very good, and it was a foggy night. The fog was very thick which made driving difficult for even the best drivers.

My dad was in the Navy and on leave he got drunk, got into a fight, and landed himself in jail. The jail was about an hour's drive from my grandparents' house.

When they heard what happened they went out to pick him up and got him out of jail. On their way home it got dark, and the fog was getting thicker. My grandfather was not a good driver at the best of times and the conditions on this night drove his anxiety through the roof.

He had a death grip on the steering wheel with white knuckles that my dad said illuminated the interior of the car. He had been following a larger vehicle for about 30 minutes with nowhere to pass and the leading vehicle was going quite slow.

Eventually the vehicle he was following stopped and just sat there. My grandfather in his angry voice said to my grandmother, "What in the name of God is that man doing stopped in the middle of the road?"

"Joe, the man is in his driveway."

For the Grandfather Who Has Everything by Bruce Miller and Team Golfwell

Question. "Grandpa, how much do you love grandma?"

"Well, even in our late sixties, that smile on her wrinkled cheeks still gives me butterflies."

– Abhinandana Rangasamy

True gems. "The old are the precious gems in the center of the household."

-- Unknown

Grandfathers become more important in their 70s. According to a scientific study, grandmothers play a major role with grandchildren during the time she is in her sixties. The research was based on 5,000 cases and found that grandfathers take the lead on guiding grandchildren after reaching 70. [6]

"Grandfathers appear to be more involved than before...grandmothers are clearly more involved with their grandchildren when a couple is younger.

However, this gender disparity gradually changes over the years. Among the oldest age groups, grandfathers usually show greater solicitude after 70... Although grandmothers spend more time with grandchildren than the grandfather, the difference in participation shrinks steadily after 60, and past 70 the grandfather usually takes the lead." [7]

Greatest compliment. "You're more trouble than the children are" is the greatest compliment a grandparent can receive."

-- Gene Perret

The majority view -- To spank or not to spank? Most grandparents view their parenting style to be superior to the parents of today. In fact, over half agree that spanking is an effective form of discipline, in comparison to 4 percent of parents who do it today. [8]

Granddad talking to his grandson: "This old pocket watch was my granddad and I got it when he died."

Grandson: "Do I get your stuff when you die?"

For the Grandfather Who Has Everything by Bruce Miller and Team Golfwell

Granddad: "Joey, that's not a polite question to ask."

Grandson: "Why not?"

Granddad: "Well it sounds like you're waiting for me to die to get my stuff."

Grandson: "I'm not waiting for you to die to get your stuff, granddad. I don't even want your stuff."

Granddad: "What's wrong with my stuff?"

I know. "Recently I was tenderly hugging one of our precious little five-year-old granddaughters and said to her, 'I love you, sweetheart.'

She responded rather blandly: 'I know.'

I asked, 'How do you know that I love you?'

'Because! You're my grandfather!'"

– Russell M. Nelson, Religious leader, and surgeon.

Old age. When you finally reach the point where you know a lot more than you did about life when you were younger, you begin to forget everything you know.

-- Unknown

Magical. "Something magical happens when parents turn into grandparents. Their attitude changes from "money-doesn't-grow-on-trees" to spending it like it does."

    -- Paul Linden

AARP Study. The AARP did a recent study. "Collectively grandparents spend a total of $179 billion per year on their grandchildren, approximately $2,562 per grandparent. Those dollars are going toward a variety of expenses and spending choices, the survey found, from gifts to education and day-to-day costs.

"Since 2001, the number of grandparents has grown by 24%, from 56 million to 70 million. By age 65, 96% of Americans are grandparents. Four in ten grandparents work, contributing to their strength as a significant market force.

"The AARP survey revealed that while grandparents make important financial contributions to their grandchildren, they also share wisdom and guidance. Many say they relish giving advice on everything from health to education, thereby providing a moral compass as well as emotional and social support." [9]

For the Grandfather Who Has Everything by Bruce Miller and Team Golfwell

Patience. "One thing you always taught me, grandfather, is patience is better than anything. That there is no reason to rush in life, and better things come with patience."

– Nicole Gopher Mampuy

Anybody's grandparent. "A child needs a grandparent, anybody's grandparent, to grow a little more securely into an unfamiliar world."

— Charles and Ann Morse

Gross humor. John visited his 90-year-old grandpa who lived way out in the country.

On the first morning of the visit, John's grandpa prepared a breakfast of bacon and eggs. John noticed a film-like substance on his plate, and asked, "Are these plates clean?"

His grandpa replied, "They're as clean as cold water can get them. Just go ahead and finish your meal."

For lunch, Grandpa made hamburgers. Again, John was concerned about the plates, as his plate appeared to have specks of dried egg on it. "Are you sure these plates are clean?" he asked.

Without looking up, Grandpa said, "I told you before, those dishes are as clean as cold water can get them!"

Later, as John was leaving, his grandpa's dog started to growl and wouldn't let him pass.

John said, "Grandpa, your dog won't let me get by!"

Grandpa yelled to the dog, "Cold Water, go lie down!"

Grandparents Piano Escape. Little Ben came into the house with a new harmonica. 'Grandpa, do you mind if I play this in here?'

'Of course not, Ben. I love music. In fact, when your grandma and I were young, music saved my life.

'What happened?'

'Well, it was during the famous Johnstown flood. The dam broke, and when the water hit our house, it knocked it right off the foundation. Grandma got on the dining room table and floated out safely.'

'How about you?'

'Me? I accompanied her on the piano!

Grandparents who babysit live longer. Grandparents who babysit grandkids live longer than same-age adults without child-rearing responsibilities, according to a study, which looked at 500 adults ages 70 and older.

The study showed that grandparents who babysat regularly had a 37 percent lower mortality risk than adults who did not.

Researchers suspect this has something to do with staying mentally active and having a purpose.

Although your kids may make you feel like you're aging rapidly, the opposite is true for your parents and in-laws, and the fountain of youth is just a sippy cup. [10]

Pappy. "Definition: Another term for grandfather, only cooler, way cooler. See also, 'handsome', 'brilliant', 'legendary.'"

    -- Unknown

What did he say? "My 2-year-old grandson has trouble pronouncing his 'Ts' 'Rs' and 'Ps'. He saw a dump truck (he loves trucks) and yelled, "Dumb F**k!"

-- Anon.

Less competition. My grandfather once told me that there are two kinds of people: those who work and those who take the credit. He told me to try to be in the first group; there was less competition there.

-- Indira Gandhi

Grandpa joke. My grandpa told me, "All you kids do these days is play video games. When I was your age my buddies and I went to Paris; we went to the Moulin Rouge and I f#*ked a dancer on stage, we didn't pay for our drinks all night and when the bartender complained we pissed on him."

After hearing this story, the grandson goes to Paris and to the Moulin Rouge with his friends. He comes back three days later with a broken arm and covered in bruises.

The grandfather asks, "What the hell happened to you?"

The grandson says "I did just like you did. I went to the Moulin Rouge with my friends; I tried to f#ck a dancer on stage and piss on the bartender - but they beat the sh#t out of me and stole all the cash in my wallet!"

The grandfather asks, "Well who the hell did you go with?"

"My friends from school, who did you go with?"

The grandfather says, "Well... the 2nd SS Panzer Division."

I would go back if... "I would love to go back and travel the road not taken, if I knew at the end of it I'd find the same set of grandkids."

— Robert Brault

True grandfather story. "My grandfather was getting to be a little senile and having some dementia problems, but we took him out for his birthday to a fairly nice restaurant regardless. The waitress came by and asked him what he wanted, and he replied, "Well I'd like a warm body, yours would do, but I think I'll have the ravioli."

-- Anon

Grandparent v. parent. "So, who's in charge, the parent or grandparent? Experts say it's the parent's job to parent unless grandparents are told otherwise, according to Stanford Children Health." [11]

"The grandparent's role is not to challenge but to fit in with the family culture," says J. Lane Tanner, M.D., associate clinical professor of pediatrics at the University of California-San Francisco. "Parents delegate authority to the grandparent, not the other way around."

Good communication and problem-solving skills are keys to healthy family relations. Criticizing or judging the way parents handle a situation can undermine their authority. This can be particularly harmful when done in front of your grandchildren.

Listen to what parents say and keep an open mind. Instead of reacting defensively, learn why your children do things a different way." [12]

Pirate! The average man will bristle if you say his father was dishonest, but he will brag a little if he discovers that his great-grandfather was a pirate.

    -- Bern Williams, Philosopher

Inspiration. "More and more, when I single out the person out who inspired me most, I go back to my grandfather."

– James Earl Jones

Grandpa's advice. "Growing old is mandatory but growing up is optional."

-- Walt Disney

Silly riddles for grandkids. How do you know when there is an elephant under your bed?

A. "When your nose touches the ceiling," he replied.

Q. Which of your grandfather's boys are not your uncle?

A. Your dad

Q. A grandfather told his grandson that he was a brave soldier in World War I. He said that he was awarded an engraved sword reading, "Proudly presenting to the hero of World War I". The grandson says you are lying. Why?

A. Simple. World War I would not be called World War I until World War II occurred years later.

Q. Why are grandfathers like parking spaces?

A. The good ones are already taken.

Q. What do grandfathers in the South have in common with lefthanded people?

A. They are both called "Southpaws."

Q. If you ask your grandfather, "What on TV?" What might he answer if it hasn't been cleaned for a while?

A. Dust.

Bargain. "What a bargain grandchildren are! I give them my loose change, and they give me a million dollars' worth of pleasure."

— Gene Perret

Who me? "I don't spoil my grandkids, I'm just very accommodating."

-- Unknown

For the Grandfather Who Has Everything by Bruce Miller and Team Golfwell

"My grandfather is the king, my dad's the prince. I guess that makes me the butler."

-- Adam Petty. Professional racing driver. He is the fourth generation from the Petty family to drive in the highest division of NASCAR racing. He is believed to be the first fourth-generation major driver in modern American professional sports.

Laughter. "Laughter is timeless. Imagination has no age. And dreams are forever."

-- Walt Disney

Age is not about how old you are. It's about how many years of fun you've had."

– Matt Maldre

A rosy outlook. "People with a rosier outlook live longer and have fewer heart attacks and depression than more negative people. One study found that thinking positively about getting older can extend lifespan by 7.5 years. And that's after accounting for things such as gender, wealth, and overall health.

A rosy outlook may help you exercise more and eat better. And that, in turn, helps you stay hopeful and happy because you feel better. You may hear that called a "virtuous circle."

If you see the glass half full, it could play an even bigger role in living better and longer than things such as low blood pressure and cholesterol, which have each been shown to increase life span by about 4 years.

You can learn to be optimistic, and it just takes time and practice.
13

Very frugal. An overly frugal grandson calls the local newspaper office to print death news of his grandpa.

Clerk: $50 per word…

Bad grandson: Grandpa Dead.

Clerk: Sorry Sir, Minimum 5 words required…

Bad grandson: "Grandpa Dead, Wheelchair for Sale."

For the Grandfather Who Has Everything by Bruce Miller and Team Golfwell

Grandfather not on the Ark? My sister's eldest boy liked nothing better than to sit on his grandfather's knee and have stories read to him. One day after a story about Noah's ark, and how Noah led pairs of animals to the safety of the ark.

The little boy asked, 'Granddad, you are very old, were you in Noah's ark?'

"Gosh no," said Granddad.

In that case, how come you didn't drown when the flood came?

-- Unknown

Doesn't fall far from the tree. Grandson: "I don't think I'm very smart, Grandpa."

Grandpa: "Oh don't say that. Hey, you're my grandson, aren't you?"

Grandson: "Yeah."

Grandpa: Well, the apple doesn't fall far from the oak tree!"

Grandson: "Grandpa, oak trees don't grow apples."

Grandpa: "See I told you you're smart!"

For the Grandfather Who Has Everything by Bruce Miller and Team Golfwell

Be silly. "Being a grandparent means you can be as silly you want to be."

– Unknown

Funny story. "My girlfriend's grandpa is in his early 70's and loves to joke - about everything (almost always sexual). So, one day I, my girlfriend, and her grandma are sitting in the kitchen at her grandparents' house and her grandpa walks in with a pair of sweatpants on with the pockets hanging out.

Grandma laughs and says to us, "Look! It looks like elephant ears."

Grandpa looks down at his pants, and without missing a beat, looks up and says, 'Wanna see the trunk?'"

Grandfather's Memory. James, a young boy of 6, turned to his grandfather and says, "When you die, Grampy, I don't want your money. Please will you leave me your memory."

-- Unknown

For the Grandfather Who Has Everything by Bruce Miller and Team Golfwell

Grandpa's Computer Memory. "My grandfather has recently started a course called 'Computers for the Terrified.' He's nearly eighty and, although used to be an engineer within the US Air Force, he is completely stuck when it comes to computers.

He came back from his first evening at this course. When asked how it had gone, he replied, 'Yes, it was really good. I really enjoyed it, but I really couldn't get to grips with my mole.'

I stopped for a second, completely puzzled until I realized he was talking about the mouse."

    -- Unknown

Need something. "Young people need something stable to hang on to — a culture connection, a sense of their own past, a hope for their own future. Most of all, they need what only a grandpa and grandma can give them."

    – Jay Kesler, Chancellor, and current President Emeritus of Taylor University

I asked my grandpa. "After 65 years you still call grandma darling, beautiful and honey. What's the secret?"

Grandpa: "I forgot her name 5 years ago and I'm scared to ask her."

    -- Unknown

Call me Jane! The AARP found in a recent study that "a strong majority (73%) of the grandparents surveyed enjoy their role and rate their performance as high, up from 66% in 2011. In addition, most say they believe their parenting skills are better than those of today's parents.

While many grandparents embrace their traditional roles, the way they relate to and engage with their grandchildren is evolving as social attitudes and technology change. For example, while most still answer to "grandma" and "grandpa," one in twenty prefers to be called by their first name. [14]

The secret to a good marriage. It was Grandparents' Day at school. "Johnny, please come up here and tell the class your story about your grandparents," the teacher asked.

Johnny stood up and began. "Good morning, everyone. My grandpa is a very wise man. He has the answer to everything. He has been married for almost 50 years now. So, I asked him, what was his secret?"

He looked at me, thought a bit, and began. "Johnny there's only one single thing to a good marriage..."

The whole class seemed to hold their breath. Everything seemed to stand still.

"And when I find out what that is, I will get married again."

An observation. "We are always the same age inside."

-- Gertrude Stein

Acceptance. "Our young grandchildren accept us for ourselves, without rebuke or effort to change us, as no one in our entire lives has ever done, not our parents, siblings, spouses, friends — and hardly ever our own grown children."

— Ruth Goode

Underestimate. "Don't ever, ever underestimate the will of a grandfather. We're madmen, we don't give a damn. Grandfathers got here before you and they will be here after you. We'll make enemies, we'll break laws, we'll break bones, but you will not mess with the grandchildren!"

— President Josiah Bartlet (Martin Sheen), The West Wing

"Grandchildren don't stay young forever, which is good because Pop-pops have only so many horsey rides in them."

— Gene Perret

Generations. "Every generation revolt against its fathers and makes friends with its grandfathers."

— Lewis Mumford, Historian

Grandson. "There are fathers who do not love their children, but there is no grandfather who does not adore his grandson."

— Victor Hugo

"Grandfathers know a lot. I know this because I am a grandfather and I feel like I know a lot of things, and frankly I'm rarely wrong."

– Blaine Pardoe

New entertainer. A man volunteered to entertain patients in assisted living homes and hospitals and brought along his portable keyboard so he could go to their rooms instead of having them gather.

As he entered the first room, he greeted an old man who lived there. He told his jokes, played his tunes, but there was no response from the very quiet old man. As he left, he said goodbye and ended with, "I hope you get better."

He was nearly out the door when he heard the old guy reply, "I hope you get better, too."

Sweet irony. "A baby has a way of making a man out of his father and a boy out of his grandfather."

— Angie Papadakis

Two things. "What are the two things your grandpa doesn't like about you as a little boy?

One, you don't want to sleep in the afternoon.

Two, you won't let him take a nap either."

-- Unknown.

What is the funniest thing you heard your grandparents say? "My nan and grandad had been married for 60 years, so I asked her, 'What was the secret to a long happy marriage of 60 years?'

Nan responded with, 'I couldn't tell you. I've been pissed off for 59 of them.'

I could not contain myself. Hilarious."

-- Anon.

Only my grandfather would say this. "My 100-year-old grandfather was revived despite him having a "Do Not Resuscitate" that is, what commonly is called a DNR.

When he achieved consciousness, he looked the EMT squarely in the eye and said, "What the hell? Are you sure you're supposed to be doing this?"

-- Anon.

My aunt told me a story about my granddad. When she was in high school, she planned to bring her new boyfriend over to meet them and granddad was given a long list of what not to ask him, "Don't ask him about his family, his grades, his job, his hobbies, etc..."

So, when he arrives my granddad shakes his hand and asks, "So.... have you ever been in prison?"

-- Anon.

A few silly riddles for grandkids.

Q. Why did grandpa's origami business go out?

A. Because it folded.

Q. What did grandpa call the movie "Avatar"?

For the Grandfather Who Has Everything by Bruce Miller and Team Golfwell

A. Smurfs for the grown-ups.

Q. What becomes shorter when you add two letters to it?

A. Shorter.

Q. Why did dad put wheels on grandpa's rocking chair?

A. Because grandpa wanted to Rock-n-Roll.

Q. What happens when a boy, his father, and grandpa laugh so hard they pee their pants?

A. You get to know that it runs in their jeans.

Q. Why did Grandpa get banned from the zoo?

A. Because he had a lion's heart.

For the Grandfather Who Has Everything by Bruce Miller and Team Golfwell

Q. Why did grandpa like to wear glasses while collecting takeout for dinner?

A. He goes to pick up the dinner with a contact-less drive-through.

Q. What did grandpa say after reading 'Karaoke Tonight' at a restaurant?

A. He just asked what sort of fish that was.

Q. What does grandpa do when you tell him to change his hearing aid?

A. He doesn't listen.

Q. Why is grandpa always smiling at grandma?

A. Because he cannot hear anything she says and doesn't want to upset her.

Learning from granddad "Life is a country that the old have seen, and lived in. Those who have to travel through it can only learn the way from them."

-- Joseph Joubert

My eyes! "Unfortunately, my grandparent's house burned in a house fire one night. It was horrible, and most of my family turned out the next day to help them. My 90-something grandmother was standing in the front yard telling my cousin and me the story of what had happened the night before. "Then your grandaddy ran out in nothing but his thongs!"

(She was referring to his shoes, but the visual was still more than I was ready for.)

-- Anon.

A hug. "Some moments can only be cured with a big squishy grandpa hug."

For the Grandfather Who Has Everything by Bruce Miller and Team Golfwell

— Dan Pearce, Single Dad Laughing

A grandson remembers. "During a family dinner, my grandfather leaned over to me and said, "Do you know what a two-timer is?"

I said 'yes'.

He said "You know... I'm a two timer."

Pretty confused at this point I asked, "What do you mean?"

He pulled up his sleeve and showed me his watch. He then pulled up his other sleeve and revealed a second watch. Nothing could've prepared me for that, I was laughing for days!"

-- Anon.

Grandfathers are books. "In this huge western culture our teaching elders are books. Books are our grandparents!"

— Gary Snyder, Practice of the Wild

Grandfather breaks world records while raising money for charities. Jack Reynolds is an inspiration to his family and holds 4 world records. He is the oldest person to perform as a supporting artist on a TV show where he had a cameo on the set of British soap named, Hollyoaks.

He also holds the record for the oldest person to receive their first tattoo (his name and DOB on his 104th birthday in 2016.

In 2017 on his 105th birthday, he rode the "Twistosaurus" in Flamingo Land, Malton, UK that made the world record for the oldest person to ride a non-inversion rollercoaster.

On his 106th birthday, he broke the record by becoming the oldest person to ride a zip wire (zip line), earning him a well-deserved spot in Guinness World Records 2019.

Jack does these to raise money after losing his wife to a cerebral hemorrhage, and the funds he raises go to the Stroke Association. [15]

Do what you have to do. "My grandfather used to take hunting trips in northern Ontario with his buddies for weeks at a time. The area they hunted was in the middle of absolutely nowhere and only accessible by helicopter.

One time, shortly after they were dropped off, their buddy started showing signs of appendicitis. They knew that this guy needed to get medical attention immediately or his appendix could rupture, and he could die.

After trying to signal for help for quite some time they ran out of options, so they tied him down, got him drunk, and prepared to cut him open and perform the surgery with their hunting/fishing equipment. Right before they were about to cut, a plane flew overhead that they were able to signal. They got their friend to a hospital just as his appendix was rupturing and he lived to tell the tale.

Grandfathers help a lot. And that has been proven scientifically.

According to Dona Matthews Ph.D., "In many ways, grandparents are ideally suited to supporting their grandkids in developing their abilities into gifts and talents." [16]

Dr. Matthews says grandparents play a major role in helping grandchildren develop their talents and confidence in society by encouraging them to pursue their interests.

"Grandparents may be the best persons in their life to ask the important questions and support them in developing their curiosities and interests into abilities. They help them take those interests farther especially when they build on their own interests." [17]

Aging. "Getting old is like climbing a mountain; you get a little out of breath, but the view is much better!"

    - Ingrid Bergman

Fountain of Youth. "There is a fountain of youth: It is your mind, your talents, the creativity you bring to your life and the lives of the people you love. When you learn to tap this source, you will have truly defeated age."

    -- Sophia Loren

For the Grandfather Who Has Everything by Bruce Miller and Team Golfwell

Grandfather knows. My grandfather was in the Navy and met my grandmother once at a dance. She wasn't particularly interested in him, but it was expected that young cute girls danced with the servicemen because they were protecting the country.

Before leaving, he got her address and said he would write to her and write he did! He wrote her very often, and according to my grandma, he had the most beautiful cursive she'd ever seen.

After a series of letters exchanged, he asked her to marry him. That's right, they met once, and he was that sure he wanted to marry her.

My grandma said yes for a couple of reasons. She wanted to get married as a lot of young girls do, it was a different time and female jobs were less common and least expected.

They got married and stayed together until my grandfather passed away when I was 2 after 40 years of marriage.

Grandfather during his life happened to drop in on my dad at his job in a shopping mall. My future mom passed by, and my grandfather said, 'That's the girl you are going to marry.'

My dad was like "Yeah right dad," but my grandpa insisted and bought a box of chocolates and made my dad give it to her and ask her on a date. My dad and mom have been married for 20 years now.

Laughter and tears. "The history of our grandparents is remembered not with rose petals but in the laughter and tears of their children and their children's children. It is into us that the lives of grandparents have gone. It is in us that their history becomes a future."

  -- Charles and Ann Morse

Like God. "My 4-year-old grandson was visiting one day when he asked, 'Grandpa, do you know how you and God are alike?'

I stood up straight and stuck my chest out while I asked, 'No, how are we alike?'

'You're both old' he replied."

  -- Unknown

"Old black-eyes" My grandmother and grandfather both grew up in Hoboken with Frank Sinatra. Frank, well before becoming famous, was known to boast about how one day he would be a great singer.

My grandparents were around 16-17 at the time of this story. They were waiting in line for a movie, and in those days, you didn't have huge theatres. You bought your ticket before the show and then waited in line outside of the theatre.

While my grandparents were waiting, up comes Frank and a few of his friends. My grandma was gorgeous! Like, movie star gorgeous. Frank had taken a liking to her, but she and my grandfather were crazy for each other.

Frank came up, and in front of my grandfather, started hitting on grandma! Now, they all grew up in the same neighborhood, so everyone was aware that my grandparents were a couple, especially Frank.

My grandfather didn't say a word. Just let him go on being a douche. Now everyone in line was paying attention.

Grandpa didn't flinch. He just rolled up his sleeves, and POW, right in the kisser. Frank hit the pavement, out cold. People applauded, and nobody helped him up. That is why, in our family, we refer to him as "Old black-eyes."

-- Anon.

Feelings grow. "The feeling of grandparents for their grandchildren can be expressed this way, "Our children are dear to us, but when we have grandchildren, they seem to be dearer than our children were."

-- Henry Old Coyote

Multiculturalism. The times they are a changin'. "Currently, one-third of grandparents surveyed have grandchildren of a different race or ethnicity than their own.

"Grandparents who have a grandchild of a different race or ethnicity say it is important to help their grandchildren learn about the heritage they share.

In addition, seven in ten try to help their grandchildren learn about the heritage they do not share." [18]

Sad? "The best place to be when you're sad is Grandpa's lap."

-- Unknown

Raising a family. "My grandfather did a lot of things in his life. What he was most proud of was raising his family."

— Tagg Romney, grandson of George Romney

Provider. My grandfather was a provider. Work, any kind of work, was the joy of his life. So, I grew up having a certain relationship to work. It was something that I always wanted.

--Al Pacino, raised by his mother and grandparents in the Bronx. [19]

Wedding reception story. "At my wedding to my first wife, we had a bunch of my old punk rock friends in attendance. Also present was my wife's very conservative grandfather. He generally expressed displeasure with her choice of a fiancé and usually was short with me.

I found him to be a bit humorless as well. Anyhow, one of my guests shows up with bright blue hair wearing only a slip and combat boots. She loudly announces that because she was living in her car, this is the best she could come up with.

Later in the ceremony, my friend rushes the garter belt throwing portion of the evening but does a mock performance with the bright blue hair. He let her slip ride up to reveal she's got nothing on underneath.

Everyone's a bit mortified, and then I hear my wife's grandfather say to her grandmother, 'Well, now we know she's not a natural bluehead.'"

-- Anon.

Granddad is honest. I phoned my grandparents and my grandfather said, 'We saw your movie.'

'Which one?' I asked.

He shouted 'Betty, what was the name of that movie I didn't like?

-- Brad Pitt

It's no surprise more and more grandparents are going online. Many grandparents feel it's vital to connect with their grandchildren because it gives them a mental and emotional boost. The AARP study found, more than 75% of grandparents are online contacting their grandkids. They don't use the phone much as they did in past years.

"Grandparents increasingly adopt new technologies, such as group texting and video chats...Although traditional media remains a relevant resource, grandparents also welcome online media sources for grandparenting information because they know that, ultimately, the more emotional support grandparents and grandchildren give each other, the happier and healthier they all will be." [20]

Living. "It matters not how long we live but how."

    -- Philip James Bailey

Reincarnation. My grandfather (who died 2 weeks ago) said, "When I die, I want to come back as a bird, there are a TON of people I want to shit on"

    -- Anon.

Indian Chief. "My grandfather always told this story to us whenever we came to visit.

He had gotten a colonoscopy and was laying on the bed in the hospital. He didn't see anyone around, so he farted really loudly. A nurse walked in right that moment.

My grandfather apologizes and the nurse replied, "It's alright. It means your body's working properly. That's a real feather in my cap."

To this my grandfather responds, "Stick around, I'll make you an Indian chief."

Next generation. "The strength of human instinct seems to be quite overrated as it is so feeble it requires a lifetime of guidance, education, training, and practical experience to develop.

More critically, without conscious and diligent effort across one generation to pass its knowledge on to the next generation, all that was gained will be lost, forewarned by an increasing rarity of the reminiscence, "Every secret of life I know, I learned at my grandfather's knee."

— T.K. Naliaka

Ideas to pass on that don't get old. Roman emperor Marcus Aurelius served as emperor 161 – 180 AD and was also a philosopher who admired and wrote about his father, grandfather, and great grandfather in a book titled Book I of "The Meditations." He wrote interesting thoughts on what they did for him and might be an ancient general source of things to consider passing on to grandchildren. Here are brief excerpts,

"I learned from my grandfather, Varus, to use good manners, and to put restraint on anger.

"I owe it to my great-grandfather that I did not attend public lectures and discussions but had good and able teachers at home; and I owe him also the knowledge that for things of this nature a man should count no expense too great.

"I learned from my father gentleness and undeviating constancy in judgments formed after due reflection; not to be puffed up with glory as men understand it; to be laborious and assiduous.

"He taught me to give ready hearing to any man who offered anything tending to the common good; to mete out impartial justice to everyone; to apprehend rightly when severity and when clemency should be used; to abstain from all impure lusts; and to use humanity towards all men.

"I observed his zeal to retain his friends without being fickle or over fond; his contentment in every condition; his cheerfulness; his forethought about very distant events; his unostentatious attention to the smallest details; his restraint of all popular applause and flattery.

"Father was tolerant of the censure of others in affairs of that kind. He was neither a superstitious worshipper of the Gods, nor an ambitious pleaser of men, nor studious of popularity, but in all things sober and steadfast, well skilled in what was honorable, never affecting novelties.

"As to the things which make the ease of life, and which fortune can supply in such abundance, he used them without pride, and yet with all freedom. He enjoyed them without affectation when they were present, and when absent he found no want of them.

For the Grandfather Who Has Everything by Bruce Miller and Team Golfwell

"He was a man of ripe experience, a full man, one who could not be flattered, and who could govern himself as well as others.

"He took regular but moderate care of his body, neither as one overly fond of life or of the adornment of his person, nor as one who despised these things…

"He carefully observed the ancient customs of his forefathers, and preserved, without appearance of affectation, the ways of his native land. He was not fickle and capricious, and loved not change of place or employment…

"He was far from being inhuman, or implacable, or violent; never doing anything with such keenness that one could say he was sweating about it, in all things he reasoned distinctly, as one at leisure, calmly, regularly, resolutely, and consistently.

"To be strong in abstinence and temperate in enjoyment, and to be sober in both—these are qualities of a man of perfect and invincible soul."

    -- Marcus Aurelius (121 – 189 AD), from Book I "The Meditations"

Just kidding! I'm very proud of my gold pocket watch. My grandfather, on his deathbed, sold me this watch.

    -- Woody Allen

Realization. "A friend of mine was asked how he liked having his first great-grandchild. 'It was great,' he replied, 'until I suddenly realized that I was the father of a grandfather!'"

-- Robert L Rice, M.D.

Having fun. Grandfathers are not old. He's just been having fun longer.

-- Unknown

House Rules for Grandfathers.

- Grandchildren welcome!
- Parents by appointment only.
- Expect to be spoiled.
- What happens here stays here.
- Storytelling.
- Play lots of games.
- Sleepovers welcome!
- Bedtime negotiable.
- Kitchen open 24 hours.
- Dessert comes first.
- Always have fun.
- Share family traditions.

-- Unknown

Grandpop. "The perfect man. Expert advice giver. Always encouraging and supportive. Biggest hug giver. Always available. Professional grandchild spoiler, and always right because he is... 'grandpop'. Basically, the best person in the whole world."

-- Unknown.

Triumph. "To keep the heart unwrinkled, to be hopeful, kindly, cheerful, reverent -- that is to triumph over old age."

-- Thomas Bailey Aldrich

Question. "Grandpa, how old are you?"

Answer. "Age is simply the number of years the world has been enjoying you!"

The Definition of a Gentleman. (My grandfather)

The definition of a gentleman is clear to detect,

it's one of warmth love and respect.

For the Grandfather Who Has Everything by Bruce Miller and Team Golfwell

When you're feeling low, grandfathers understand,

like they have the answers in the palm of their hands.

To the warmth of their smile from the shake of their hand,

that says more than words ever can.

I'm not talking about pulling out chairs or opening doors,

it's the knowledge that you're never far from their thoughts.

With wings of hope, they will always catch you,

if money was love, they'd make you richer.

I think we should learn to be just like

these beautiful human beings.

    -- Anon.

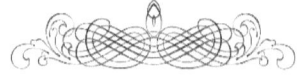

For the Grandfather Who Has Everything by Bruce Miller and Team Golfwell

Index to paragraphs

A Gentleman 1

Age to me means nothing 1

Practical joke reversed 1

Baby wonderment 2

If I'd known 2

Awesome grandchild 2

You just know. 3

Boo! 3

Patience. 4

-- 4

Memories 4

Hands. 4

House rules 5

"I love this child… 5

Kicked it 6

Grandpa's ears 6

Lots of fun 6

No control 6

A brief and interesting history of grandfather 7

Strong will 8

For the Grandfather Who Has Everything by Bruce Miller and Team Golfwell

Lots of energy 8

Magician 9

Grandpa is texting his son. 9

Always have time. 10

A grandpa wedding story 10

Grandpa and Teen texting 10

Blend 11

Frugal 11

Happy Anniversary! 11

A perfect blend. 12

Ripping advice 12

Grandpa Poem 12

Am I a bad grandpa? 14

Miss him 14

Rolex. 14

No regrets 15

If it's breaks – get grandpa. 15

10 again. 15

It was grandpa's 100th birthday 16

Revolt 16

Ask Grandma 16

For the Grandfather Who Has Everything by Bruce Miller and Team Golfwell

Wrong one!...17

Rodney Dangerfield 17

What did you do in the old days? 17

No glasses 18

Made by God...18

The wait is over...19

Walk the walk 19

Dentist office...19

Stories 20

Horses 20

What grandfathers do 21

Paying attention...21

How old are you? 22

How the heck did I get this old!..22

A joke...22

Story keepers..23

Transition 23

Distance?..23

Grandchildren survey 24

Experience..25

Influence...26

For the Grandfather Who Has Everything by Bruce Miller and Team Golfwell

No thank you. 26

Close friends. 26

True story 26

Seriously. 27

Antiques 27

Self-respect. 27

Grandfathers just know. 28

Got to go. 28

God does have a sense of humor 29

Sounds. 29

Granddad joke 29

Giving them a sense of identity 29

Meaning. 31

Riddles for smart grandkids. 31

Grandfather goes out for an afternoon bicycle ride. 33

Definition of FUNPA 33

Experience. 34

How many grandparents are in the US? 34

What children need most 35

Nature's way. 35

Some warm thoughts. 35

For the Grandfather Who Has Everything by Bruce Miller and Team Golfwell

Grandkids remember grandpa's diet. 36

On the other side of the coin. 38

Identity 38

Friend 38

Choosing grandpa names. 39

A philosophical view of maturity 41

Outrageous stuff. 41

Beaten to death 42

Forever young 43

Magic happens. 43

Teen is amazed 43

Love grows with age 43

The average age of grandparents is on the rise 44

Getting older. 44

Special place. 45

Well, now that I think about it. 46

Perfect, of course! 46

You know you're a grandpa when… 46

Grandma's game 47

It's in the genes. 47

A granddaughter's story 47

For the Grandfather Who Has Everything by Bruce Miller and Team Golfwell

Advise 49

Consolation from the strong 49

Having a grandpa 49

Tell me a story 49

Smoking 50

Hindsight 50

Exceptional 50

Reaching out 50

Youthful inside 51

Pouring whiskey 51

Grandma's confession 51

Feel loved 51

Grandparents' kissing and hugging 52

Reflections 53

Let me tell you about my grandchildren! 53

My dad told me this story about my grandfather. 54

Question 55

True gems 55

Grandfathers become more important in their 70s 55

Greatest compliment 56

The majority view -- To spank or not to spank? 56

For the Grandfather Who Has Everything by Bruce Miller and Team Golfwell

Granddad talking to his grandson 56

I know. 57

Old age 57

Magical 58

AARP Study 58

Patience. 59

Anybody's grandparent 59

Gross humor 59

Grandparents Piano Escape. 60

Grandparents who babysit live longer 61

Pappy 61

What did he say? 62

Less competition 62

Grandpa joke 62

I would go back if… 63

True grandfather story 63

Grandparent v. parent 64

Pirate! 64

Inspiration 64

Grandpa's advice 65

Silly riddles for grandkids. 65

For the Grandfather Who Has Everything by Bruce Miller and Team Golfwell

Bargain. 66

Who me? 66

"My grandfather is the king 67

Laughter 67

Age is not about how old you are 67

A rosy outlook 68

Very frugal 68

Grandfather not on the Ark? 69

Doesn't fall far from the tree 69

Be silly. 70

Funny story 70

Grandfather's Memory 70

Grandpa's Computer Memory 71

Need something 71

I asked my grandpa 71

Call me Jane! 72

The secret to a good marriage 72

An observation 73

Acceptance 73

Underestimate 73

"Grandchildren don't stay young forever 74

For the Grandfather Who Has Everything by Bruce Miller and Team Golfwell

Generations. 74

Grandson 74

"Grandfathers know a lot. 74

New entertainer. 74

Sweet irony. 75

Two things. 75

What is the funniest thing you heard your grandparents say? 75

Only my grandfather would say this. 76

My aunt told me a story about my granddad. 76

A few silly riddles for grandkids. 76

Learning from granddad 79

My eyes! 79

A hug. 79

A grandson remembers. 80

Grandfathers are books. 80

Grandfather breaks world records. 80

Do what you have to do 81

Grandfathers help a lot 82

Aging. 82

Fountain of Youth 82

Grandfather knows 83

For the Grandfather Who Has Everything by Bruce Miller and Team Golfwell

Laughter and tears 83

Like God 84

"Old black-eyes" 84

Feelings grow. 85

Multiculturalism. 85

Sad? 86

Raising a family 86

Provider. 86

Wedding reception story 86

Granddad is honest 87

It's no surprise more and more grandparents are going online 87

Living. 88

Reincarnation 88

Indian Chief. 88

Next generation 89

Ideas to pass on that don't get old 89

Just kidding! 91

Realization 92

Having fun. 92

House Rules for Grandfathers 92

Grandpop 93

For the Grandfather Who Has Everything by Bruce Miller and Team Golfwell

Triumph 93

Question 93

The Definition of a Gentleman 93

We hope you enjoyed our book! 106

About the authors 106

Bruce Miller 106

TeamGolfwell 106

We Want to Hear from You! 107

Other Books by Team Golfwell and Bruce Miller 108

References 109

We hope you enjoyed our book!

If you liked our book, we would sincerely appreciate your taking a few moments to leave a brief review.

Thank you again very much!

TeamGolfwell and Bruce Miller

About the authors

Bruce Miller. Lawyer, businessman, world traveler, golf enthusiast, and Golf Rules Official, actor, shrewd gambler, whiskey connoisseur, and author of over 35 books, a few being Amazon bestsellers, spends his days writing, studying, and constantly learning of the astounding, unexpected, and amazing events happening in the world today while exploring the brighter side of life. He is a member of Team Golfwell, Authors, and Publishers.

TeamGolfwell are bestselling authors and founders of the very popular 200,000+ member Facebook Group "Golf Jokes and Stories." Their books have sold thousands of copies including several #1 bestsellers in Golf Coaching, Sports humor, and other categories.

We Want to Hear from You!

"There usually is a way to do things better and there is opportunity when you find it." - Thomas Edison

We love to hear your thoughts and suggestions on anything and please feel free to contact us at
Bruce@TeamGolfwell.com

Other Books by Team Golfwell and Bruce Miller

Brilliant Screen-Free Stuff to Do with Kids: A Handy Reference for Parents & Grandparents!

For the Golfer Who Has Everything: A Funny Golf Book

For the Mother Who Has Everything: A Funny Book for Mother

For the Father Who Has Everything: A Funny Book for Father

For the Grandmother Who Has Everything: A Funny Book for Grandmothers

Dragonflies: A Novel Based on What Men Think of Women

The Funniest Quotations to Brighten Every Day: Brilliant, Inspiring, and Hilarious Thoughts from Great Minds

Jokes for Very Funny Kids (Ages 3 to 7): Funny Jokes, Riddles and More

Jokes for Very Funny Kids (Big & Little): A Treasury of Funny Jokes and Riddles Ages 9 - 12 and Up

And many more here

References

[1] My goodtime stories, https://mygoodtimestories.com/2015/07/11/grandchildren-can-say-they-funniest-things/

[2] AARP, https://www.aarp.org/home-family/friends-family/info-2018/grandparenting-quiz.html#quest1

[3] Dr. Eugene Beresin M.D., M.A., Psychology Today, https://www.psychologytoday.com/us/blog/inside-out-outside-in/202005/the-value-being-grandparent#:~:text=Grandparents%

[4] Grandparents National Survey, https://www.aarp.org/content/dam/aarp/research/surveys_statistics/life-leisure/2019/aarp-grandparenting-study.doi.10.26419-2Fres.00289.001.pdf

[5] Xu, Jiaquan et al. Mortality in the United States, 2015. NCHS Data Brief No. 267. Washington, DC: Centers for Disease Control and
Prevention, December 2016.

[6] Science Daily, https://www.sciencedaily.com/releases/2012/11/121105081621.htm

[7] Ibid.

[8] "Parenting in America: Outlook, worries, aspirations are strongly linked to financial situations." Washington, DC: Pew Research Center,
December 17, 2015.

[9] AARP, https://www.aarp.org/research/topics/life/info-2019/aarp-grandparenting-study.html

[10] Fatherly referencing research, https://www.fatherly.com/health-science/scientifically-backed-benefits-grandmas-grandpas/

[11] Stanford Children Health, https://www.stanfordchildrens.org/en/topic/default?id=let-your-children-raise-their-kids-1-2281
[12] Ibid.
[13] WebMD, https://www.webmd.com/healthy-aging/healthy-aging-secret
You can learn to be optimistic. It just takes time and practice.
[14] Supra, AARP
[15] Guinness World Records, https://www.guinnessworldrecords.com/news/2020/3/daredevil-grandpa-breaks-record-every-year-for-his-birthday-610491
[16] Dona Matthews Ph.D. Psychology Today, https://www.psychologytoday.com/us/blog/going-beyond-intelligence/202105/grandparents-and-giftedness-talent-and-creativity
[17] Ibid.
[18] Supra, AARP
[19] Wikipedia, https://en.wikipedia.org/wiki/Al_Pacino
[20] Supra, AARP

www.ingramcontent.com/pod-product-compliance
Lightning Source LLC
Chambersburg PA
CBHW021428070526
44577CB00001B/118